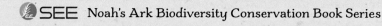

SEE

The Fish Of
the Jinsha River

Written by Tan Deqing and Xiao Jin   Illustrated by Bai Song and Shi Nianlu

Preface

The Southwest Project Center of the Alashan Society of Entrepreneurs & Ecology (SEE) initiated a program in 2013 for biodiversity conservation of the alpine forests in China's mountainous Southwest. Named SEE Noah's Ark, it is financed by the SEE Foundation in Beijing. Multiple conservation projects have been implemented by working with various stakeholders to protect endangered and rare species of flora and fauna, especially those with extremely small populations. It adopts solutions inspired by nature and advocates participation by the community, encouraging protection and the sustainable use of local biological resources.

The stories in the SEE book series: *The Asian Elephant*, *The Yunnan Snub-Nosed Monkey*, *The Green Peafowl*, *The Fish of the Jinsha River*, and *The Himalayan Honeybee*, all come from true experiences of front-line rangers and locals in conservation action. They are incredible. For both nature's characters and the people in the story, their connection to the native land and affection towards each other is rarely heard and miraculous in their own way. We then came up with a proposal to compile these lovely stories in a picture book to all our friends who have supported SEE conservation projects. They can be linked to real characters from dense woods and remote mountains, where heart touching stories occurred due to their generous support.

This picture book series is a group of works by conservation workers, scientists, sociologists, writers, and artists. The characters, environment, and neighboring creatures have all been carefully selected from real situations in our projects. In addition, explanatory notes of conservation are made to enrich the reading experience. We hope you enjoy it!

We extend our respects to those who have worked so hard to conserve their natural homeland, as well as to the SEE members and public who give donations to support these projects. These volumes are our gifts for the United Nations Biodiversity Conference COP15 held in Kunming.

XIAO JIN
Secretary of the SEE's Southwest Project Center
Chairperson of the SEE Noah's Ark Committee
June 2021

Data File: Fish of the Jinsha River

Name in Chinese	圆口铜鱼 (YUANKOUTONGYU)	Family	Cyprinidae
Name in English	Largemouth bronze gudgeon	Subfamily	Gobioninae
Alternate Names	Gold loach, diver fish, beardfish, old-sow fish, square-head, fat bay fish, pockmark fish, round-mouth	Genus	*Coreius*
		Species	*Coreius guichenoti*
Latin Name	*Coreius guichenoti*	Distribution	Main Middle Yangtze tributaries; Wuchang; Wujiangdu; Mudong (Chongqing); Yibin; Panzhihua; Lijiang; Mianning
Kingdom	Animalia		
Phylum	Chordata		
Subphylum	Vertebrata		
Class	Actinopterygii	Authorship	Sauvage et Dabry, 1874
Order	Osteichthyes	Conservation Status	Critically Endangered

Distribution and Conservation Areas in China

City / Autonomous Prefecture	County / District	River	Conservation Area / other notes
Wuhan	Wuchang	Middle Yangtze	—
Yueyang	Chenglingji	Middle Yangtze	—
Yichang	Yiling	Middle Yangtze	—
Zunyi	Wujiangdu	Wu River, Upper Yangtze Tributary	—
Chongqing	Wanzhou	Upper Yangtze	—
Chongqing	Mudong	Upper Yangtze	—
Luzhou	Hejiang	Upper Yangtze	Upper Yangtze Conservation Reserve for Rare and Unique Fish
Yibin	Cuibing	Lower Jinsha River	Upper Yangtze Conservation Reserve for Rare and Unique Fish
Xichang	Mianning	Ya Long River, Middle Jinsha Tributary	—
Panzhihua	East District	Middle Jinsha	—
Dali	Heqing	Middle Jinsha	—
Lijiang	Gucheng	Middle Jinsha	—
Lijiang	Yulong	Tiger Leaping Gorge, Middle Jinsha	Uppermost Distribution for Largemouth Bronze Gudgeon

Yuanyuan is a tiny fish egg, transparent and shining. She was laid and fertilized among cobbles in the turbulent currents of the Jinsha River, upstream of the Yangtze River. Yuanyuan and thousands of fish eggs, her sisters and brothers, begin their drifting journey at birth.

♂ Male

♀ Female

Fertilized egg

2

Among them, only a few lucky ones can hatch and get through the torrents, eventually growing to their full size. Will Yuanyuan be the lucky one?

The Fish of the Jinsha River

The largemouth bronze gudgeon is a rare species, native to the Jinsha River, which is classified as endangered species. It is a kind of fish that hatches eggs out to drift. The spawning period is from late April to early July. The most upstream for spawning reaches Daju Township at the outlet of the Tiger Leaping Gorges, Jinsha River, and at most downstream on the Yangtze River, around Pingshan, Yibin, Sichuan. After fertilization, the eggs absorb water and soon expand to a size as large as soybeans. They start to drift in the currents for about 48 hours and develop into fries. After 4–5 days, as the swim bladder and fins have developed, the largemouth bronze gudgeon begins to swim freely.

Yuanyuan could not wait, gulping down a mouthful of water and expanding. She broke through her egg membrane and started tumbling and bumbling among the rapid waves. She soon developed into a fry. With her swim bladder, Yuanyuan tried dances of all kinds on the waves and felt novelty all around.

SPLISH!

SPLISH!

SPLISH!

4

Suddenly, a huge carp opened its big mouth and swallowed most of her siblings around her. Coincidently, a whirlpool happened to sweep Yuanyuan away from that mouth, saving her life.

HELP!

The Fish of the Jinsha River

Such omnivorous fish as carp and crucian carp, often prey on eggs and fries. They are the "number one killers" of native species in the Jinsha River. Alien species, such as catfish, leather beards, and scavengers, released by humans into high-altitude rivers and lakes of the Jinsha River, threaten the native species.

Yuanyuan continued to drift down the river, tumbling and trembling with fear all the way. She adjusted her body and directed herself with the newly emerged fins. She tried to paddle and drag her gradually elongated body, diving under the turbulent surface water to avoid all kinds of ferocious big fish.

One day, Yuanyuan was whirling around a small vortex, playing with the newly grown tail. In a surprise, waves of small fish came around her. Yuanyuan swam back and forth among them, looking at her new companions. Among them were her kind of largemouth bronze gudgeon and also crucian carp, silver carp, Zong fish, Guan fish, blunt snout bream, silver catfish, horse-mouth fish, loach, catfish, freshwater eel, Chinese sturgeon, Manli eel and mandarin fish, etc.

Ya-Fish (*Euchiloglanis kishinouyei*)

Clear-cut-mouth split belly fish (*S. Prenanti*)

The Fish of the Jinsha River

There are eight fish nurseries in the middle and lower reaches of Jinsha River, to introduce man-assisted reproduction. They will adopt such help to spawn, incubate and then release the fries of rare or endangered fish into the river, thereby increasing their populations. This is a relatively new means to restore the ecosystem, balanced with biodiversity.

On her journey down the river, Yuanyuan made new friends on the way: the mullet, the bronze gudgeon, the long-fin Wenju fish, and various loaches. The new friends happily went together and carried on southeastward, heading to the warm and rich waters of the middle Yangtze.

Suddenly, a tall dam appeared in front of them, blocking their way.

The Jinsha River has rapid flows, with a large drop and plentiful water resources. From the Tiger-leaping Gorges to Yibin in Sichuan, there are now 12 hydropower stations. These hydropower stations provide clean energy for mankind, but they cut off waterways between the upstream and downstream, which harms the fish. In order to build a passage for migrating fish, major hydropower stations are required to build fishways, a man-made tunnel for fish to pass through the dam. This facilitates gene exchange and encourages genetic diversity amongst a large number of fish.

"Want to get across the dam?! Come with me!" said a crucian. All youngsters followed, sliding down a long ladder.

"So exciting. I want to go again!"

"There are plenty of big dams ahead. We're lucky to find such a slide – it's a red carpet passage for fishes!"

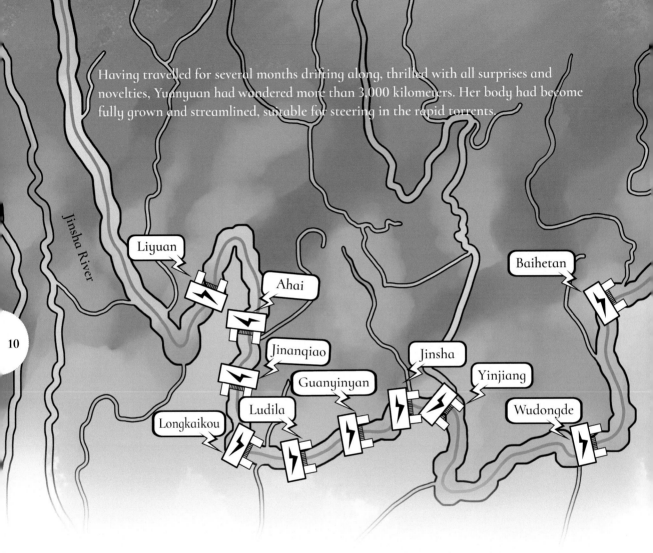

Having travelled for several months drifting along, thrilled with all surprises and novelties, Yuanyuan had wandered more than 3,000 kilometers. Her body had become fully grown and streamlined, suitable for steering in the rapid torrents.

Jinsha River

Liyuan

Ahai

Baihetan

Jinanqiao

Jinsha

Yinjiang

Guanyinyan

Wudongde

Longkaikou

Ludila

10

Yuanyuan had passed through several dam slides and for every journey she would say goodbye to some friends. Some of them had decided to stay in rivers, lakes and reservoirs on the way because they were sedentary for a certain Grea.

Yibin (Yangtze)

Xiluodu

Xiangjiaba

Yuanyuan kept moving eastwards merrily, saying farewell to old friends and making plenty of new ones on the journey. She joined a troop of new friends like the mullet, Chinese sturgeon, Chinese paddlefish and Yangtze sturgeon. They struggled through their tough journey and finally reached the wide Yangtze River!

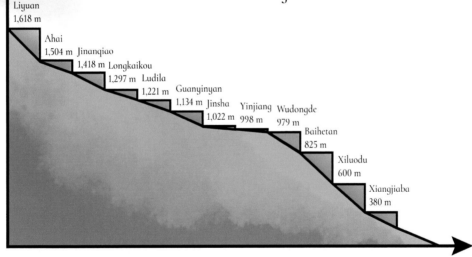

To the Tiger Leaping Gorge

Elevation

Liyuan
1,618 m

Ahai
1,504 m Jinanqiao
1,418 m Longkaikou
1,297 m Ludila
1,221 m Guanyinyan
1,134 m Jinsha
1,022 m Yinjiang Wudongde
998 m 979 m
Baihetan
825 m
Xiluodu
600 m
Xiangjiaba
380 m

11

The Fish of the Jinsha River

The Jinsha River flows through the four provinces and autonomous regions of Qinghai, Tibet, Sichuan and Yunnan, with a total length of 2,331 km. The watershed area covers about 340,000 square kilometers and drops by 3,300 m in elevation (Zhu Kezhen, 1981) along the entire route. The whole river is generally split into three sections, the upper section from Yushu to Shigu (length 984 km, average drop of 1.75%), a middle section from Shigu to Panzhihua (564 km in length, average drop of 1.48%), and a lower section from Panzhihua to Yibin (783 km in length, average drop of 0.93%).

Heigh-ho!

Three years later, Yuanyuan was an adult fish. People have several nicknames for largemouth bronze gudgeon, like the gold loach, dive-down fish, beard-fish, and old-sow fish.

She had become an experienced soldier by now, having learnt how to live in the river bottom currents. She was omnivorous, eating river bugs, shellfish, shreds of plant, fish eggs and fries, too.

One day, on a long journey searching for food, Yuanyuan smelt something good approaching the surface. She could see the other fish fighting amongst each other to grab some titbits just on the top. She was to rush up for a bite. Suddenly there was a flash of silver light, a huge fish-net tightened up, and trapped fish. Luckily, Yuanyuan escaped from the very bottom of the net.

12

Another night, just before she started to feel sleepy, Yuanyuan suddenly saw a streak of white light.

"Quick! Quick! Get out of the way! It's pulse fishing!" yells a huge fish, swimming past.

Luckily, Yuanyuan stayed in the depths most of the time. The rock ridge at the river bottom helped shelter her from the pulse.

CRACKLE!

CRACKLE!

13

But Yuanyuan was terrified to see a whole crowd of her companions upturned and floating on the surface. Even those big and bold fish could not be spared.

Yuanyuan had survived again!

The Fish of the Jinsha River

Overfishing, illegal fishing, and water pollution have become the main causes of endangered species and the decline of the wild fish population along the Yangtze River. Pulse-fishing is illegal and the greatest threat among all these unlawful activities.

Cruising and growing in the warmth of the Yangtze, Yuanyuan was to become a mother. Once she carried eggs, she knew that it was time for her to depart for an upstream home journey. She would lay her eggs in the rapids of the middle and upper Jinsha, just as her own mother had done for her.

Mullet (*Myxocyprinus asiaticus*)

Long loach

Chinese paddlefish (*Psephurus gladius*)

of the Jinsha River

Fish migration refers to the periodic directional round-trip movement of fish due to physiological, genetic, and external environmental factors. Migration is a long-term adaptation of fish to the environment. It enables the species to adopt more favourable resources and better reproduction. In the natural flows, the largemouth bronze fish spawning in the Jinsha River requires about 200–300 km of river length.

Yuanyuan's home journey wasn't an easy one. The way was long and she hurried up with no delay. She swam upstream day and night, along with many companions on the same spawning migration. With friends, Yuanyuan felt a bit relaxed. She was to make it back to the Jinsha River.

Mullet (*Myxocyprinus asiaticus*)

Glug! Glug!

Chinese sturgeon (*Acipenser sinensis*)

There are about 400 fish species in the Yangtze River. Among them, 350 are freshwater fish, ranking top for river fish varieties in China. In addition, there are about a dozen types of sea-river migratory fish. Among them are seven upstream migrating kinds, such as Chinese sturgeon (*Acipenser sinensis*), Chinese paddlefish (*Psephurus gladius*), Yangtze sturgeon (*Acipenser dabryanus*), mullet (*Myxocyprinus asiaticus*), bronze gudgeon (*Coreius heterodon*) and a shad, going upstream for spawning in the Jinsha. The others like the Manli eel (*Anguilla*) and Songjiang perch are downstream migration types that could be sea-bound spawning fish.

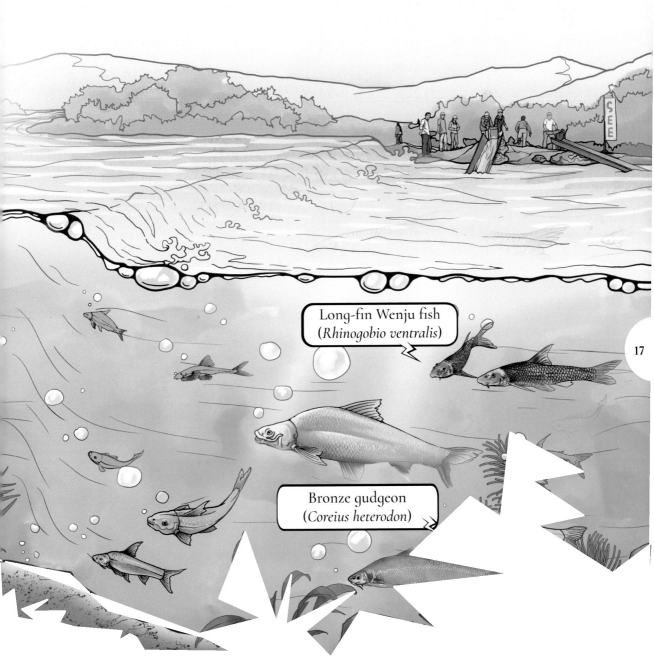

Long-fin Wenju fish
(*Rhinogobio ventralis*)

Bronze gudgeon
(*Coreius heterodon*)

17

Yuanyuan was now back at the dam. She had some vague memory about the excitement of sliding down the fish path of dams, one after another, when she was little.

Now for her to go upstream against the current, it seemed not possible at all. Yuanyuan turned round and round again at the foot of the dam. Her spawning time was approaching day by day. What should she do?

Sichuan split belly fish (*Schizothorax kozlovi*)

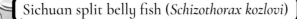

The Fish of the Jinsha River

Fishways, fish locks, fish elevators, fish boats, and net fishing over the dam are facilities to help migratory fish pass through the hydropower station. But the effectiveness differs in circumstances. The fish tunnel is suitable for low and medium-faucet water control projects. With high dams or cascade development on rivers, fish passing facilities are not viable to help migrating upstream fish in terms of fish species conservation. Currently, fish resources are mostly protected by man-assisted reproduction, or by making use of natural and man-built spawning grounds around the dam.

Chinese paddlefish (*Psephurus gladius*)

Chinese sturgeon (*Acipenser sinensis*)

Luckily, the troubled Yuanyuan met an old largemouth bronze gudgeon. It told Yuanyuan: "I was also born in the middle reaches of Jinsha River, like you. I tried and couldn't go back either. I therefore laid eggs nearby, and my children grow well here."

Following the old lady's guidance, Yuanyuan and her partners found the cobbles under the river by swimming around. She laid her first batch of eggs. These eggs were to be fertilized in gushing water and develop into fries. Tens of thousands of transparent and shiny eggs began their drifting life from here, carrying Yuanyuan's hopes and blessings.

Yangtze sturgeon (*Acipenser dabryanus*)

The Fish of the Jinsha River

All kinds of fish are particular about their spawning circumstances, such as water temperature, water flow, water quality, light, and substances nearby. In places conducive to reproduction and embryonic development, fish will breed in large groups, forming a spawning ground. This is the result of fish adapting to the environment in the long-term survival process.

About the Authors

Tan Deqing is a researcher at the Institute of Hydrobiology, Chinese Academy of Science. He has published many papers and monographs.

Xiao Jin is a retired scholar at the Chinese University of Hong Kong. She participated in environmental protection after retirement and was appointed vice president and secretary-general of the SEE Conservation Project Center and president of the SEE Foundation. She also led in establishing the SEE Noah's Ark Project.

About the Illustrators

Bai Song has a Master's degree in engineering and has engaged in art education work for many years. She is now vice president and professional leader of Yunnan Light and Textile Industry Vocational Collage. She has edited and published two national planning textbooks, one jewelry major series teaching material for vocational institutes, and many educational, teaching, and research-related papers in relevant academic journals.

Shi Nianlu, born in the 1990s, is an experienced designer who graduated from the visual communication department of Yunnan Arts University. In her five-year design career, she gained rich experiences and developed professional design and aesthetic ability. She was the executive designer for many exhibitions, including the Suwen series, Afterwards the recommended exhibition of young artists, and Endless Poetry the Tianfu Painting exhibition.

SEE Noah's Ark Biodiversity Conservation Book Series

SEE: The Fish of the Jinsha River

Written by Tan Deqing and Xiao Jin
Illustrated by Bai Song and Shi Nianlu

First published in 2023 by Royal Collins Publishing Group Inc.
Groupe Publication Royal Collins Inc.
BKM Royalcollins Publishers Private Limited

Headquarters: 550-555 boul. René-Lévesque O Montréal (Québec) H2Z1B1 Canada
India office: 805 Hemkunt House, 8th Floor, Rajendra Place, New Delhi 110 008

Original Edition © Yunnan Science & Technology Press Co., Ltd.

ISBN: 978-1-4878-1080-1

To find out more about our publications, please visit www.royalcollins.com.